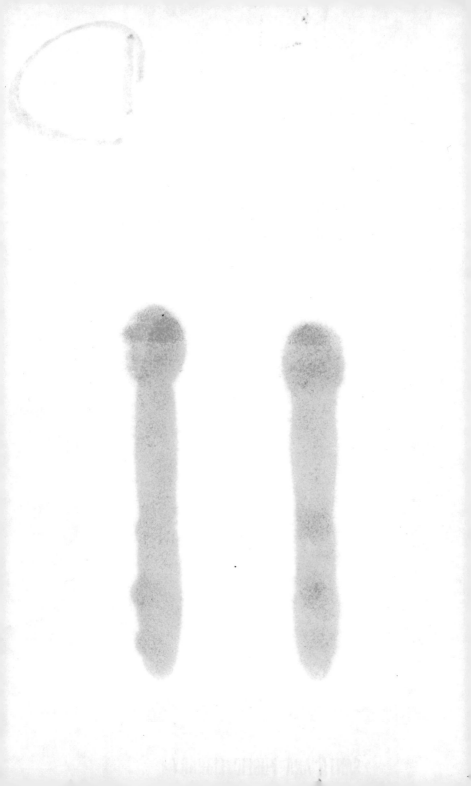

Art Tells a Story: Greek and Roman Myths

Art Tells a Story: Greek and Roman Myths

🀫🀫🀫🀫🀫🀫🀫🀫🀫🀫🀫🀫🀫🀫🀫

Penelope Proddow

WITH AN INTRODUCTION BY ELIZABETH FLINN,
IN CHARGE, THE JUNIOR MUSEUM AT
THE METROPOLITAN MUSEUM OF ART

DOUBLEDAY & COMPANY, INC.
GARDEN CITY, NEW YORK

Library of Congress Cataloging in Publication Data

Proddow, Penelope.
    Art tells a story.

    1. Mythology, Classical, in art—Juvenile literature.
I. Title.
N7760.P74   704.94′7′0938
            ISBN 0-385-11111-8 Trade

            0-385-11112-6 Prebound
    Library of Congress Catalog Card Number 76–18363

Dedication

About six years ago, I started to catalogue a collection of engraved gems. Most people think immediately of heads and portraits. However, this collection also included mythological scenes. As engraved gems were so small and costly, they followed the major art trends of their day and, in cataloguing them, I discovered that the telling of Greek and Roman myths had continued from ancient times down to the present.

Later, when I was asked to lecture in the Junior Museum at The Metropolitan Museum of Art, I chose to lecture on the Greek and Roman myths, not on the gems but on the larger works of art which had inspired them. These spanned the centuries and included all media; and the story illuminated them for young and old alike. The series of lectures turned into the weekly program, "Art Tells a Story."

Once again a shift has been made. What began as a catalogue of cameos and intaglios, what grew into the lecture program "Art Tells a Story," has now been put into a book. I cannot express enough gratitude to those who have helped along the way: to Louise Condit for her kindness in setting up the program in the Junior Museum; to Elizabeth Flinn for her encouragement and guidance in developing it; to Margaret Nolan and her staff for their patience in finding just the right slides and transparencies; and finally to Raphael and Ralph Esmerian, through whom I first learned that art tells a story. To them this book is dedicated.

PENELOPE PRODDOW

New York, 1977

Contents

Author's Note

The names of the characters in these stories are both Greek and Roman, as they have been taken from the titles of the works of art in which they appear. The Romans enjoyed the Greek myths and in their re-tellings gave their own names to the gods and goddesses, such as Bacchus, Diana, Venus, and Cupid.

Introduction

Penelope Proddow's programs in the Junior Museum are designed for children and their parents to learn about and enjoy the collections of The Metropolitan Museum of Art. After hearing Miss Proddow tell the story of a work of art through slides, Museum visitors of all ages eagerly search for the original in the galleries, often sketching what they find.

The Junior Museum is delighted that some of the stories are now available to a wider audience through this book, *Art Tells A Story: Greek and Roman Myths*. The art, life, and beliefs of the ancient Greeks and Romans come alive through the dramatic stories and vivid illustrations.

I hope these stories will stimulate readers to look carefully at, think about, and enjoy many works of art and discover that from ancient times to the present, art has told the story of a people, place, and time.

Elizabeth H. Flinn
In Charge, The Junior Museum
The Metropolitan Museum of Art

Art Tells a Story: Greek and Roman Myths

Athena, Perseus, and Medusa

🮲🮲🮲🮲🮲🮲🮲🮲🮲🮲🮲🮲🮲

PLATE I

Long ago, there was a Greek princess, Danae, whose father locked her up in a tower. He had heard that she would bear a mighty son, and he was afraid this son would overthrow him. As a result, Danae had no suitors—except Zeus, the king of the gods. Zeus changed himself into a shower of gold and came through a crack in Danae's window. She bore him their son, Perseus.

Enraged, Danae's father put her and the baby in a box, which he threw into the sea. The box came to rest on an island where a kindly fisherman opened it and took the two into his cottage. They would have stayed there with him forever had not his brother, the king of the island, come on a visit. He was as evil as the fisherman was kind.

This wicked king wanted to marry the princess. He would have forced her to marry him right away, but he was afraid of Perseus who was now sixteen years old and very strong. So, he sent the boy off on a quest for the head of Medusa, who lived at the other end of the earth. Anyone who looked at Medusa was instantly turned to stone.

Perseus, however, was not without friends. After all, he was the son of the king of the gods. Athena, the goddess of wisdom and duty, came to help him immediately. She outfitted him with gifts from the other gods: a winged hat to make him invisible, winged sandals to take him through the sky, and a hooked sword to cut off Medusa's head.

Away Perseus went. He came upon the monster at the end of the earth. Athena, the goddess of wisdom and duty, appeared at his side. He looked at her, as he reached for the Medusa's head. He never knew that the monster was a beautiful girl, sleeping on a flowery hillside. If he had, he might have looked away from his goddess, away from wisdom, and away from duty. He might have looked at Medusa, done nothing, and been turned to stone like the heroes before him.

As it was, he took the head and returned to the island. He turned the evil king to stone and went on to perform even greater deeds—without the head of Medusa. Athena took that as her prize and wore it ever after on her shield.

This Greek vase is called an Attic red-figure vase. The words "Attic" and "red-figure" describe a place and a style. The clay for this vase came from a part of Greece called Attica. The painter outlined the figures on the clay with a black line, added details to their

PLATE I. "Athena, Perseus, and Medusa" painted by Polygnotos. Red-figured pelike. Attic, ca. 450–40 B.C. The Metropolitan Museum of Art, Rogers Fund, 1945.

PLATE II. "Bacchus punishing Eastern kings for opposing introduction of vine." Ivory pyxis, front and back view. Sixth century. The Metropolitan Museum of Art, Gift of J. Pierpont Morgan, 1917.

PLATE III. "Hector and Andromache" from *The Destruction of Troy*. Wool and silk tapestry, 15′7½″ x 8′9½″. Franco-Flemish, fifteenth century. The Metropolitan Museum of Art, Fletcher Fund, 1939.

PLATE IV. "Diana and Actaeon." School of Pellipario. Maiolica dish. Diameter: approximately 8″. Castel Durante, ca. 1520–25. The Metropolitan Museum of Art, Samuel D. Lee Fund, 1941.

PLATE V. "The Birth of Cupid." School of Fontainebleau. Oil on wood, 42½" x 51⅛", ca.,1540–60. The Metropolitan Museum of Art, Rogers Fund, 1941.

PLATE VI. "The Feast of Acheloüs" by Peter Paul Rubens and Jan Brueghel, the Elder.
Oil on wood, 42½" x 64½"; with added strips 43⅛" x 65¼". The Metropolitan Museum of

PLATE VII. "Midas Bathing in the River Pactolus" by Nicolas Poussin. Oil on canvas, 38⅜" x 28¹/₁₆". The Metropolitan Museum of Art, Purchase, 1871.

PLATE VIII. Harpsichord supported by Tritons, with gilded gesso relief showing processions of Galatea. Accompanying gilded figures of Galatea and Polyphemus playing a bagpipe inflated by bellows. Italian, seventeenth century. The Metropolitan Museum of Art, the Crosby Brown Collection of Musical Instruments, 1889.

PLATE IX. "Pygmalion and Galatea" by Jean Léon Gérôme, 1824–1904. Oil on canvas, 35″ x 27″. The Metropolitan Museum of Art, Gift of Louis C. Raegner, 1927.

PLATE X. "Leda" by Paul Gauguin, 1889. Lithograph on zinc, printed on yellow paper and heightened with water color. From a series of eleven. 11 15/16″ x 10 3/16″, Circle: diameter 8 1/16″. The Metropolitan Museum of Art, Rogers Fund, 1922.

PLATE XI. "Pandora" by Bertrand Jean Redon (called Odilon), ca. 1910. Oil on canvas, 56½" x 24½". The Metropolitan Museum of Art, Bequest of Alexander M. Bing, 1959.

PLATE XII. "Study for Prometheus" by Kurt Seligmann. Pen and India ink, 23^{15}/₁
x 28^{15}/₁₆". The Metropolitan Museum of Art, Gift of Walter C. Baker, 1967.

bodies and clothes in black, and painted the rest of the vase the same color. As a result, the figures stand out in the original red of the clay against a black background.

The red-figure style is admired for two reasons. First, the figures retain a skin color which makes them seem very real. Secondly, they move dramatically against such a stark background.

This vase was painted in 450 B.C. at the height of Attic red-figure vase painting. The artist was able to draw the human body in various positions and he was able to create a mood. Here Athena is standing. Perseus is moving forward in a running position. Medusa is lying down. Athena is also thinking: she is waiting for Medusa's head. Perseus is acting: he is looking back at his goddess as well as wielding his hooked sword. Medusa is sleeping, unmindful of her power, her beauty, and her danger. So, the artist, the painter Polygnotos, has used his knowledge of the way human beings move to create a gripping adventure story. Because of this, he is considered one of the masters of Attic red-figure vase painting.

Polygnotos was part of a long tradition of Greek vase painters. Traces of their styles may still be seen on his vase. The pattern of Medusa's skirt recalls a style called the Geometric style, when triangles, squares, and zigzags covered the entire surface of a pot. The flowers around Medusa recall another style called the Orientalizing style, when flowers, vines, and fabulous animals from the East wound around the surfaces of pots, vases, and perfume bottles. In 450 B.C., however, Polygnotos used these motifs sparingly,

Athena and Perseus. Detail from "Athena, Perseus, and Medusa." Red-figure pelike painted by Polygnotos.

Medusa. Detail from "Athena, Perseus, and Medusa." Red-figure pelike painted by Polygnotos.

as details to enhance a skirt or to highlight the expanse around the neck and handles.

Polygnotos wrote "Perseus" above his hero's head. Not everyone in the ancient world knew their Greek mythology. They liked Greek vases for their shapes and practicality. This red-figure vase is a pelike, a container for wine, and its broad shape makes it almost impossible to tip over. A host might take out a pelike such as this for a party. On one side the story of Perseus, Athena, and Medusa would appear. Guests would pour their wine and stay to read the title "Perseus" and follow his story.

One guest might start the conversation by exclaiming: "Look at the rays of light around Perseus' helmet! Is that symbolic of his divine birth?" He did begin his life in a burst of light and enthusiasm. Though the brilliance of those rays has flaked away, Perseus is a child of the gods as well as a man of action on this Attic red-figure pelike painted in 450 B.C.

The Triumph of Bacchus

ᓚᓚᓚᓚᓚᓚᓚᓚᓚᓚᓚ

PLATE II

Long ago, the god Bacchus went on a trip to the East to introduce his new plant, the grapevine. He made the journey in a chariot drawn by spotted leopards instead of horses.

Unfortunately, Bacchus' trip turned quickly into a warlike expedition. Nobody in the East had ever heard of the grapevine, and nobody wanted to learn anything about it. In fact, the kings of Syria and India were so much against it that they sent out whole armies to stop Bacchus.

Bacchus, however, had his own devoted band of followers. They were called satyrs. These creatures had the hooves and horns of goats and the bodies of men. Usually they carried shepherd's crooks to herd their sheep and goats. But in time of battle, they swung these staffs over their heads suddenly and brought them down like clubs. They used their horns and hooves as well. Then they grabbed their foes by the hair, as if they were unruly animals, and flung them down to the earth.

Needless to say, the well-trained Eastern armies had never faced a god in a leopard-drawn chariot, and they had never fought satyrs. They were surprised, astonished, and terrified. They fled in confusion, tripping over the wine cups which held the juice of the vines. In the end they were beaten roundly.

Bacchus advanced through the East triumphantly, and his leafy plant, the grapevine, sprang up everywhere in the wake of his chariot.

This small, round ivory box was cut from a section of an elephant's tusk. It is called a pyxis. In Greek and Roman times, ivory pyxides were used most often to hold jewelry, but this particular pyxis came from a country in the East, probably Syria, and had a different use.

In the sixth century A.D., Syria was one of the great trading centers. Here ideas for works of art were exchanged. Roman artists usually told about the spoils the god Bacchus brought back from his expedition to the East. Naturally, the later Syrian artists told what he brought *to* the East—the grapevine by the wheels of his chariot.

Although this Syrian artist must have seen the Roman artists' works, he told the story in his own way. First, he carved Bacchus and his followers on just one or two planes. He left blank spaces between the fighting figures. As a result, there are lights and shadows on the ivory box, which give a feeling of drama to the battle that continues around the pyxis.

A Satyr. Detail from "Bacchus punishing Eastern kings . . ."
Ivory pyxis.

Secondly, Eastern artists were fond of animals and vines, and this artist has made them an important part of the story. Here Bacchus' leopards have distinct spots. They pull hard within their harness. By the wheels of the rushing chariot grows a single, leafy plant. It is the sturdy grapevine, which was supposed to have changed the East from a desert into a green garden.

So, the Syrian artist has taken a Roman myth and carved it in his own Eastern style. Afterward, someone took his pyxis with its depiction of a pagan god and put it into a Christian church to hold wafers for the Mass. Did anyone notice the subject? Or had Bacchus become a part of Syrian history? After all, he had brought the vine to the East long before the coming of Christianity.

Hector and Andromache

𐃘𐃘𐃘𐃘𐃘𐃘𐃘𐃘𐃘𐃘𐃘𐃘

PLATE III

Long ago, there was a very great city on the coast of Asia Minor called Troy. The king and queen of this city had many sons and daughters. One of their sons carried off a beautiful Greek girl named Helen. The Greeks were so enraged that they gathered together a huge army and sailed over the sea to bring her home. With that, the Trojan War, the famous battle between the Greeks and Trojans, began.

The Trojan War went on for nine long years. Many of the king and queen's sons died, but their favorite, a warrior named Hector, still lived. Then one day, Hector's wife, Andromache, had the frightening feeling, as she watched the fighting, that he, too, would die very soon. Later, on the walls of the city, she fell to her knees and begged him not to go back into battle. But Hector would not listen. He put on his helmet. He said good-by to his wife and son and entrusted them to his mother and sisters. He said a last good-by to his father at the palace gates and rode onto the battlefield.

Hector fought bravely. However, after he defeated the best friend of the strongest Greek warrior, that warrior rose up and killed him. All too quickly, Andromache's fears had come true. Hector died and Troy fell to the Greeks.

Warriors were not usually thought of as husbands, fathers, and family men, and so when a hero appeared in a legend who was both a courageous fighter and an adored husband, he was remembered. The story of Hector and Andromache was first told by the Greek poet Homer in his epic *The Illiad*. Hundreds of years later, the artists of the Middle Ages retold it in their own way, through poetry, prose, drama, illuminated manuscripts, and tapestries.

On this fifteenth-century tapestry, Hector is dressed not as a Trojan warrior, but as a Medieval knight in armor. His wife, Andromache, his mother, Hecuba, his aged father, Priam, step right out of a Medieval castle with their brocaded robes. They might be a Medieval family were it not for the names on the tapestry and the rhymed couplets, giving the story in French overhead and in Latin below.

Their costumes portray the subsequent history of the Trojan royal family. After the fall of Troy, some of Hector's brothers fled with their families over the sea and settled in Europe. They became the most powerful men of their new land. Consequently, the later European kings traced their lineage through them back to King Priam and his family.

These later European kings and their families did

Andromache, Hecuba, and Hector. Detail from "Hector and Andromache." Wool and silk tapestry.

Priam and Hector. Detail from "Hector and Andromache."
Wool and silk tapestry.

not look upon the Trojans simply as ancestors. They identified with them. Charles the Bold, a relative of the French king, owned this tapestry. The weaver, Pasquier Grenier, wove the story in the colors of Charles the Bold's shield: blue, red, and tan for the gold. Then he included the bells from Charles the Bold and Margaret of York's wedding celebrations on the harness of Hector's horse. Could the love of Charles the Bold and Margaret of York have been less than that between Hector and Andromache?

Charles the Bold and Margaret of York hung this tapestry in their castle at Bruges, which was in Flanders. It was part of a set of eleven tapestries with stories from the Trojan War. Like the other tapestries, it kept the rooms of the castle warm and bright in the winter and fluttered out the windows for parades in the spring. But, unlike the other tapestries, this one told its owner's story.

In 1476, Charles the Bold invaded Switzerland. It is thought that he took this tapestry with him to hang in his tent. The following year he died in battle. Had his wife, Margaret of York, begged him not to go just like that long-ago Trojan woman, Andromache? If so, the drama on the walls of Troy had been played out once again, not only in a Medieval tapestry, but in actual Medieval life.

Diana and Actaeon

𜰫𜰫𜰫𜰫𜰫𜰫𜰫𜰫𜰫𜰫𜰫𜰫

PLATE IV

Long ago, in the ancient world, everyone went hunting, so the king of the gods was not very surprised when his young daughter, Diana, burst into his throne room and asked to go hunting, too.

"Please, Father," she cried, "may I wear a short hunting tunic, even though I am a goddess, and carry a bow and arrow?"

She grabbed his beard before he could say no and continued, "Father, I would like a forest with shadowy groves and a city with a dancing hall and friends my own age who want to hunt and dance, too!"

"I would give a hundred cities to such a spirited daughter as you," cried her father, "a hundred forests, a fringed tunic, a bow and arrow, and a following of nymphs instead of suitors!"

Diana sped out of his throne room before he could change his mind. She gathered up her friends. All of them were nymphs, daughters of the river-god.

All of them were young. And all of them loved hunting and dancing more than anything else on earth.

From then on they spent their time racing between the shadowy groves of the forest and the dancing halls in the city. Sometimes they stopped along the way to freshen up in their favorite fountain.

One evening, just as the sky was turning the color of ripe mulberries, Diana and her friends were heading back to the city. They pulled off their tunics, their quivers, and their boots to enjoy the cool waters of the fountain by the side of the road. The hunter, Actaeon, happened to be on his way back to the city, too. He passed by the fountain and stopped to watch them.

"Diana herself!" he exclaimed. "Goddess of the hunt! Leader of the dance!"

The nymphs shrieked. They clustered around the goddess to shield her, but the goddess was taller than any of them. She was also angrier. Her bow and arrow lay out of reach on the pebbly ground, so she splashed water into the hunter's startled eyes. Suddenly his face became long and sorrowful. His ears stood up on end. They grew into antlers. He turned into a stag. His dogs chased him away from Diana's fountain and slew him far off in the hills.

This dish takes its name Maiolica from the island of Majorca in the Mediterranean Sea. In the fifteenth century, Spanish ships stopped there on their way to Italy with cargoes of glazed pottery. The Italians thought the glazed pottery had been made on Majorca and called it by the island's early name, Maiolica. They liked the pottery so much they soon learned to make it themselves.

During the sixteenth century, Maiolica painters gave the gods and goddesses of the ancient world new life. Here the goddess Diana splashes in an ornate Italian fountain. The hunter Actaeon trembles in fanciful modern dress. The painter is telling their story.

Story-telling on Maiolica pottery was called *istoriato*. This way of painting was perfected by the painter, Nicola Pellipario, who lived in the small Italian city of Castel Durante and made it famous.

Nicola Pellipario never thought of himself as anything more than a craftsman, a man who worked with his hands. He threw his clay on a potter's wheel. It went most easily into the shape of dishes and plates. He fired these in a kiln until they were very hard. This is known as the biscuit condition. He then dipped them in a tin-enameled glaze.

This glaze gave the pottery a smooth, white surface, but it drank up color very quickly. The painter had to draw on it with speed and accuracy before the colors dried. He used paints which came from metallic oxides: green from copper, yellow from rusty iron, and a famous blue from cobalt.

Since blue was the most celebrated color of Maiolica pottery, is it any wonder that Nicola Pellipario perfected the narrative style of painting, or istoriato, with heroes and heroines, gods and goddesses who were at home in the sea, sky, and even the blue waters of a fountain?

On this Maiolica dish, Diana and her nymphs

Actaeon turning into a stag. Detail from "Diana and Actaeon."
School of Pellipario. Maiolica dish.

Diana with her nymphs. Detail from "Diana and Actaeon."
School of Pellipario. Maiolica dish.

live in a dreamlike world of country roads, calm lakes, distant cities, and unexpected fountains, but the little band moves awkwardly in its surprise. They don't have the grace of Nicola Pellipario's figures. This dish was probably painted by one of his followers.

Italian princes and nobles of the sixteenth century treasured these Maiolica dishes and plates for their lively stories and bright colors. They hung them on the walls of their palaces. No one seemed to know about Greek vases with their myths as yet, but isn't it just as well? This way, painters such as Nicola Pellipario and his followers were free to pass on their own versions of the ancient stories.

The Birth of Cupid

PLATE V

Venus, the goddess of love, was born from the foam of the sea. The moment she stepped onto the beach, the four Hours and the three Graces rushed up, wrapped her in a cloak, and took her off to meet the other gods and goddesses.

Venus brought laughter and joy to heaven and afterward to earth. Everyone fell in love. As Venus gazed on the gods and goddesses who fell in love and had families, and at the ordinary people on earth who did the same thing, she decided she wanted a son.

This son was born from the earth in springtime. His name was Cupid, or Love. As soon as he was born, the four Hours and the three Graces hurried into Venus' chamber, pulled back the curtains, held up dishes of fruit and jars of sweets, and scattered pansies, roses, and cornflowers.

Then everyone gasped. The little boy was small. He was sickly. He had no joy. He had no wings. Venus went to a temple to pray to the gods, although she, too, was a goddess. The answer came, "Love cannot live without love returned."

So Venus bore a second son, whose name was Love Returned. After that, Love grew large and joyful and sprouted wings.

"The Birth of Cupid," as imagined by this unknown painter, could only have taken place in sixteenth-century surroundings similar to his own. He lived and worked at the palace of Fontainebleau, where François I, king of France, had brought painters, sculptors, architects, and masons to transform the Medieval chateau into a lavish, sixteenth-century palace. His painting may reveal not only the interior of the palace but also a very dramatic moment in one of its chambers.

Are its inhabitants human beings or gods and goddesses or one posing as the other? They are fine-boned, slender, and elegant. They wear clothes in rainbow colors. They pull their hair back in golden fillets, jewels, and flowers. They rest lightly on couches or come out of the shadows, as if they had wings.

Venus lies on a bed decorated with lion heads and pearls and covered with luxurious cushions and a light blue coverlet. Is she Venus, the goddess of love? Or is she the beloved of the king, with a newborn son? The three Graces and the four Hours rush forward in silk robes. They hold jars of fruits, sweets, and ointments and fling back the curtains to reveal either a memorable occasion in the history of the world, the birth of Cupid, or a memorable occasion in the history of the palace of Fontainebleau, the birth of a

An Hour and a Grace. Detail from "The Birth of Cupid."
School of Fontainebleau.

The Hours, Cupid, and Venus. Detail from "The Birth of Cupid." School of Fontainebleau.

son. Which is it? The art of Fontainebleau is an art which teases the imagination.

All the paintings which hung at Fontainebleau had this elegance, this lightness, this tender and sometimes pearly-white color. The obvious delight in the differing textures of woods, flowers, silken threads, and jewels reflects the actual work being done on the palace of Fontainebleau and its gardens. Since the style is unique, such paintings are called the Fontainebleau School.

The Feast of Acheloüs

᠅᠅᠅᠅᠅᠅᠅᠅᠅᠅᠅᠅᠅

PLATE VI

One day the Greek prince Theseus and his friends were on their way home from a boar hunt. They were about to cross a river, when a terrific storm broke overhead and they could go no farther.

"Come into my cave," cried the river-god, Acheloüs, "until the storm passes!"

They went inside and found it was no ordinary cave. There was a carpet of moss on the floor and a collection of seashells on the walls. There were bright birds singing in the corners and, best of all, there was a long table laden with food and drink.

The young men reached out eagerly for the food and the golden goblets, but before they could begin, the river-god pointed to an island and began a story.

"There she is—my first love!" he cried. "Once she was a beautiful princess. Her father threw her over a cliff for consenting to marry me. I called to the god of the sea and he turned her into an island outside my window!"

"Really?" said Theseus.

"I don't believe it," said one friend.

"Oh," said another. "The gods do wonderful things."

"And so do I!" cried the river-god. "I fought with the strongest man on earth for a second princess. I turned into a bull in combat and he ripped off one of my horns."

"How terrible," said one of the youths.

"Not at all," said the river-god. "I keep the horn as a souvenir. It was a wonderful fight. My girls will serve you fruit from its hollow."

The storm passed. The sun was shining brightly on the island and sunbeams were flickering through the marvelous cave, when the travelers left. They were shaking their heads, all of them, and wondering about the strange things that happened on earth.

It is hard to believe that Theseus and his friends didn't touch the seafood or drink any refreshment from the golden goblets in this painting. Nevertheless, the unwritten title of the work is "The Feast of Reason." The exchange of strange and wonderful stories is in contrast to the feast of delicious food and drink. It is two painters' recipe for a superb dinner party.

Peter Paul Rubens and Jan Brueghel the Elder worked during the seventeenth century in the rich and bustling city of Antwerp, which was then in Flanders. They found the story in *The Metamorphoses*, a book of myths by the great Roman storyteller, Ovid. Jan Brueghel painted the setting. He blended the magic of a river-god's cave with the splendor of a Flemish

The side table. Detail from "The Feast of Acheloüs" by Peter Paul Rubens and Jan Brueghel the Elder.

dwelling. The seashells over the walls of the cave are arranged exactly like those in the cabinet of curiosities of a widely traveled Flemish collector. They are also exactly like those on a real beach. The golden ewers and cups, the work of the finest Flemish craftsmen, sparkle on the side table. Underneath them is an oriental rug, the work of the finest Eastern craftsmen. These were the treasures of a Flemish home and they became the treasures of the Greek river-god's cave, a combination of natural and man-made beauty. Through it all wafted the soft music of rare birds and the sweet smell of autumn fruits and flowers. In this setting Jan Brueghel prepared a table with exotic vegetables, plump chickens, and seafood for Peter Paul Rubens' guests.

Rubens delighted in the movement of human beings. He painted Acheloüs, the nymphs, the river deities, Theseus and his friends. The nymphs and river deities bring more golden pitchers and fresh platters of food from the side table and the cold spring, even though the food already on the table has barely been touched. Theseus and his friends are twisting and turning, to catch a better view of the storyteller, his souvenirs inside and outside the cave, or to take a cup of refreshment. Their various poses match the expressions of amazement, disbelief, and wonder on their faces.

The feast of Acheloüs has been a wonderful party, as sumptuous as any the painters attended during their successful careers in Antwerp.

Even though the story was written by the Roman

Acheloüs and his guests. Detail from "The Feast of Acheloüs" by Peter Paul Rubens and Jan Brueghel the Elder.

storyteller Ovid, and even though the painting was created by two Flemish painters, no description of a good party, either in words or in images, can ever be outdated.

And so, that good host and good sport, Acheloüs, lives on, fascinating us as he fascinated Theseus and his friends long ago. Wouldn't we all like to come out of a storm and feast with him in his delightful cave?

The Story
of King Midas

𒀭𒀭𒀭𒀭𒀭𒀭𒀭𒀭𒀭𒀭𒀭𒀭

PLATE VII

There was once a very rich king named Midas, who had an enormous palace and a beautiful, cultivated rose garden.

One day, a follower of the god Bacchus happened upon this rose garden. He had never seen anything like it before. He had seen only the blossoming fields, vineyards, orchards, and flowers, which Bacchus cared for in even the smallest villages on earth. He decided to stay there but, unfortunately, he was captured by the king's gardeners.

When Bacchus heard that his follower was a prisoner of King Midas, he went immediately to the rescue. The king was very polite to him. After all, Bacchus was a god with great power and could grant him anything he desired. In return for freeing the god's follower, King Midas asked Bacchus for the golden touch, so that everything he touched would be turned to gold.

By the end of that day, King Midas had galleries of golden statues in the shape of animals, birds, and flowers. That evening, King Midas sat down at a golden dinner table. Everything continued to turn to gold when he touched it: the meat, the vegetables, the salad, and dessert. By morning, King Midas had to send for Bacchus. He was starving to death.

King Midas begged Bacchus to take away the golden touch. The god sent the king to scrub it off at the source of the river Pactolus. There, in the presence of a river-god and his bubbling sons, King Midas learned that the source of life and happiness was the water which nourished the god's kingdom: the orchards, vineyards, flowers, and fields all over the earth.

The story of King Midas is well known. The dangers of turning everything into gold are clear, but the remedy for this talent, which so quickly becomes a curse, is often forgotten. Midas had to go back to the source of life and happiness on earth before he was able to free himself from his own wish. The ending of this story is what Nicolas Poussin chose to paint.

Although Bacchus, the god of the earth, helped Midas, he himself does not appear in the painting. Pactolus, the river-god, and his two children are present instead. They wear vine wreaths, Bacchus' symbol, so Bacchus is there in spirit as Midas works frantically to wash away his golden touch.

Nicolas Poussin was a French seventeenth-century painter, who traveled as a young man to Rome and never returned to live in his native country, France.

The river babies. Detail from "Midas Bathing in the River Pactolus" by Nicolas Poussin.

He painted "Midas Bathing at the Source of the River Pactolus" just after he arrived in Rome. It is a youthful painting. The figures are arranged on a simple diagonal. First appear the river babies, who are playing with the stream and their pots of water. They are unaware of the conflicts on earth. Next, the river-god reclines on a rock and watches the efforts of a human king attempting to rid himself of all his dreams and desires, symbolized by the golden touch. The river-god's face is hidden. No one can see his emotions. At the end of the diagonal, Midas is scrubbing himself all over with the clear water of the river Pactolus.

As the observer's eye moves back toward Midas, the mystery of the scene heightens. What can be happening in the small space of wilderness, created by those looming rocks, that dark, jutting tree, and the stream? The mood is quiet and thoughtful. The colors are warm and vibrant. Poussin has roughly combined the ruddy skin tones of his characters with the rich browns of the rocks, the dark brown of the tree trunk, and the green patches of growing things. Then, he adds a silver trickle of water, the source of the river Pactolus. The bubbles downstream are caused by the two river babies. They do not need to learn where their happiness is coming from at that moment.

Beyond the characters the sky is somber. Here Poussin has not created a landscape. He has painted a backdrop. His story does not take place in a real world, but in a world of poetry and ancient mythology.

Midas. Detail from "Midas Bathing in the River Pactolus" by
Nicolas Poussin.

Polyphemus and Galatea

𓀀𓀀𓀀𓀀𓀀𓀀𓀀𓀀𓀀𓀀𓀀

PLATE VIII

Long ago, there was a sparkling young sea nymph named Galatea. She never went anywhere alone. She always traveled with her many friends who lived in the sea with her—girls called Nereids and boys called Tritons. They all swam over the surface of the waves, carrying horns and trumpets and waving crabs and little fishtails. Usually they hoisted Galatea onto a shell and carried her along behind them. Their procession became known as "The Triumph of Galatea."

On the shore a giant watched the triumph of Galatea each day. His name was Polyphemus. He was everything the Tritons were not. He was large, clumsy, and awkward. He had two legs instead of a flashing tail, and he couldn't swim. Nevertheless, he thought Galatea was the most wonderful being in the world. He took up his bagpipes and sang love songs to her.

Of course, Galatea never heard his songs. She was too busy playing with her companions or hurrying to meet the young man she loved, a shepherd who watched his herds on a lonely stretch of white beach.

Soon Polyphemus could stand it no longer. He put down his pipes and followed Galatea. He watched her swim faster and faster, and he ran along the beach to keep up with her. When he saw that Galatea was swimming to meet the shepherd, he let out a roar of anguish, gripped the top of a hill, and threw it down at his rival.

Quickly Galatea used the magic of the sea to turn the shepherd into a fishtailed being. They dove under the waves amid laughter and bubbles, leaving Polyphemus alone on the beach.

Here the Tritons and Nereids are carrying a harpsichord, which has been covered with gold and decorated with "The Triumph of Galatea." The procession of sea creatures on the harpsichord case is traveling in a different direction from the one below. The light-hearted beings carry horns, trumpets, and shells and wave crabs, turtles, and little fishes. Galatea is hardly distinct from her friends on the golden case of the harpsichord. She is not swimming below in the bluish-green waves on the base. She is not even sitting on the shell behind. A little boy perches there. He may be the god of love, the cause of the whole story.

This harpsichord group was created in Italy during the seventeenth century. At that time, changes were taking place in music. Melody became very important. In much the same way, Polyphemus and Galatea are set apart from the background of Nereids

Polyphemus. Detail from "Harpsichord supported by Tritons . . ."

Galatea. Detail from "Harpsichord supported by Tritons . . ."

and Tritons. Polyphemus, the burly, lovesick giant, sits to the left side. Galatea, the bubbling, little Nereid, sits opposite him. Like a melody, they have come out from among the mass of swirling sea creatures and tell the story.

This harpsichord group stood in the first museum of musical instruments, which was Michele Todini's Galleria Harmonica in Rome. The group stood against a backdrop of painted stucco mountains and trees, Polyphemus' seaside home.

Polyphemus' rock hides a set of silver pipes, which were played by a special keyboard beneath the harpsichord. These imitate the music of Polyphemus' bagpipes. Though he never moved, he seemed to play a love song to Galatea upon a real wind instrument. She held a lute in her arms at one time. And, though she never moved, she seemed to answer him. The delicate sounds of the harpsichord gave her dainty little reply and told better than words how unsuited the two were for each other. Nevertheless, the rough, honest sounds of the wind instrument and the gay, carefree ripple of the stringed instrument must have made a lovely melody.

Pygmalion
and Galatea

🏛🏛🏛🏛🏛🏛🏛🏛🏛🏛🏛

PLATE IX

Once there was a poor sculptor named Pygmalion. He lived by himself with his statues. Unfortunately, he could never find a woman attractive enough to marry. They were either too tall, or too fat, or too thin. So, he carved figures of women out of stone, instead. He made them just the right height and just the right weight, but when he had finished they were still only stone figures that stared at him from the shelf.

One day, he started a new statue. She was to be his masterpiece. He named her Galatea, perhaps after the lovely sea nymph. He chipped away very carefully and hoped he would never finish her.

Around that time there was a festival in the town. Everyone was going to worship the goddess of love and ask her for one wish. Pygmalion had never taken anyone to dances or to plays, but still he went to the goddess of love to make his wish.

"Could I, Goddess of Love, have a wife just like my statue?" he murmured. He didn't dare ask for his statue as a wife, but that was what he really wanted.

Afterward Pygmalion left the festival and returned to his quiet room. He walked around his statue. She was beautiful, standing there in the evening light. He couldn't help himself. He kissed her.

Out of the shadows of the artist's room flew the goddess of love's little boy, Cupid, with his bow and arrow. He loosed an arrow of love, and all the sculptor's wishes and prayers were answered. His statue came to life.

As Pygmalion kissed Galatea, her hair turned a rich brown. The blood moved through her body. Slowly she turned from marble to flesh and, when she stepped off the pedestal, Pygmalion took her back to the festival. They danced and, in the end, married happily.

Have you ever painted anything you wished would come to life? That is the secret dream of many artists. They work very hard to make the knee just right, the ankle just right, so that if the person in their painting did come to life, he or she would not fall down. These painters are called realists. They want everything they do to seem real. The French artist, Jean Léon Gérôme, was a realist and he painted "Pygmalion and Galatea" in 1881. It was a time when people were following the excavations of ancient cities, looking at statuettes in museums similar to those in Pygmalion's studio and reading myths and plays.

Jean Léon Gérôme chose the part of Pygmalion's

Pygmalion and Galatea with the painting of the festival, and the statues. Detail from "Pygmalion and Galatea" by Jean Léon Gérôme.

Cupid. Detail from "Pygmalion and Galatea" by Jean Léon Gérôme.

story in which Galatea comes to life. From Gérôme's painting it is hard to believe Pygmalion was ever very happy without her. Against the wall are some masks and a shield which symbolize the ancient myths and legends. On the floor are chips of marble, a chisel, a few crates, and a set of wooden stairs. On the shelf is a line of lifeless statues. Jean Léon Gérôme was a master of genre art—the branch of art which shows people as they really are. And he enjoyed showing people as they really were more than two thousand years ago.

With colors he becomes poetical. Nothing can equal the beautiful statue in the middle of the room. She is coming to life without a doubt. Her hair has turned a rich brown. Her neck and shoulders are turning a rosy pink. Her legs are still the color of white marble. At the base of the pedestal is a fish, symbol of the goddess of love.

Jean Léon Gérôme painted Pygmalion and Galatea in the artist's workshop. Nevertheless, he has woven in all parts of the story. On the wall is a picture of the festival. Pygmalion is kneeling at the bottom of the steps of the temple, asking for his wish. On the other side of the room, the goddess of love's little boy is coming out of the shadows with his bow and arrow. He is answering the wish.

Jean Léon Gérôme was a sculptor as well as a painter and he knew the longing to bring something to life. This may be why he signed his own name *J. L. Gérôme* at the base of the statue. Another title has been suggested, "Love Breathes Life into Sculpture," as Jean Léon Gérôme's love of color and composition breathes life into painting.

Leda and the Swan

𒀭𒀭𒀭𒀭𒀭𒀭𒀭𒀭𒀭𒀭𒀭𒀭

PLATE X

Once upon a time, in the far-off kingdom of Sparta, there was a beautiful queen named Leda. Nobody on earth had ever been so beautiful. And yet, her beauty was lost. She lived in a country of warriors and athletes, and all she ever did was walk by herself in the woods, along the river, and among the flowers.

Now, the king of the gods was lonely one day, so he looked down to earth. He saw the warriors and athletes arming themselves, throwing spears and racing chariots. Then, as his eye moved over the countryside, he saw the queen, Leda, in the woods. She was exquisite there among the trees and flowers—and all alone. The king of the gods wanted to woo her at once. He didn't dare go as a god, for no mortal could withstand the sight of a god in his full glory. But he didn't want to go as one of the warriors or athletes either. He wanted to do her beauty justice. He wanted to be part of her world of flowers and rivers and trees. In his mind's eye, he saw himself as a swan, so that was the disguise he took.

He landed on the river, courted Leda, and she fell in love with him. Later, she bore him a daughter who was hatched from a golden egg. Her name was Helen and she was the most beautiful princess on earth.

About a hundred years ago in Paris, there was great excitement over Japanese prints. The painter, Paul Gauguin, was stirred by them and decided to tell the Greek myth of Leda and the Swan in Japanese fashion.

What did Paul Gauguin admire about Japanese art? He answered the question himself by saying, "Look at the Japanese who draw so admirably and you will see there life in the open air and in the sun without shadows. . . ."

Leda is in the open air among fruits, flowers, leaves, and little forest creatures. It is a world with no shadows. The artist has written over the top "homis [*sic*] soit qui mal y pense," which means in French "evil he who evil thinks," and then his monogram, "PGO." In other words, don't look for gloom and shadows in this world. It is one of sunshine, open air, ripening fruits, and flowers.

Paul Gauguin used a black outline instead of lights and shadows to give the swan, Leda, and the forest world their forms. He printed them first on Japaneselike yellow paper. Then he added other colors by hand: pinks, whites, tans, greens. He didn't use these colors to give depth and distance to the world he was creating. He used them instead to make a flat design similar to that on a china plate. He called his Leda "Projet d'assiet [*sic*]," which means "design for a china plate," and wrote this below with the date "89" for 1889.

Leda and the swan. Detail from "Leda" by Paul Gauguin. The
Metropolitan Museum of Art, Rogers Fund, 1922.

Two ducklings. Detail from
"Leda" by Paul Gauguin.

No one could ever say that Leda walked through a real forest or that Gauguin painted her there. Here a few flowers are a garden. A leaf is a woodland. Two ducklings and a swan are a large river. A little green snake wiggles in an enchanted countryside. The part tells the whole. This is called an abstraction.

"Do not paint too much from nature," was Paul Gauguin's advice. "Art is an abstraction. Seek it in nature by dreaming in the presence of it. . . ." In other words, don't paint what you see. Shut your eyes and paint what you dream. The circle around his picture recalls the story's end, the golden egg which hatched into the beautiful princess. It also brings back the beginning, the inner eye, the mind of the god and his imaginings. The whole picture becomes a dream, not of the night, but of the day, a daydream.

The Story of Pandora

𝕔𝕦𝕣𝕦𝕔𝕦𝕔𝕦𝕔𝕦𝕔𝕦𝕔𝕦

PLATE XI

Once there were two brothers, Prometheus and Epimetheus. They lived together on earth and they
created the first men. They gave men the best of everything and they kept the bad in a box in their
house. This box contained sickness, sorrow, envy,
madness, and anything else which might make men
unhappy. As a result, everyone was very happy at this
time. In fact, there was nothing to separate men from
the gods and the gods were very distressed. So, they
created a woman.

The god of fire gave her a lovely form. The goddess of handicrafts dressed her in flowing robes. The
Graces decked her with flowers. The Hours added
herbs. The messenger-god gave her a curious nature.
At the end, they clustered around their creation,
named her Pandora which means "All Gifts," and
sent her down to earth.

Epimetheus was at home when Pandora arrived.
He welcomed her. She was lovely; she was sweet; she

was talkative. Since neither he nor his brother had created her, he didn't know she was also filled with curiosity. No sooner had she made herself at home than she lifted the top of the box and looked inside.

Sickness, sorrow, envy, madness came out with a rush. Pandora struggled to put the top back. Nevertheless, there was something unexpected at the bottom, clambering to escape, which was stronger than Pandora and stronger than anything yet on earth. It was hope. Hope sprang out, chased the ills away from that household, and pursued them into the world.

Then Prometheus and Epimetheus settled down with the gods' creation. Even though Pandora had opened their box, she far outdid the sorrow on earth with the loveliness, grace, and hope she brought to their lives.

The French painter, Odilon Redon, saw nothing dangerous about Pandora, when he painted her in 1910. On the contrary, he chose her not so much for her curiosity or for the troubles she loosed on the world, as for her beauty and the gifts the gods gave her. Some of these gifts, such as flowers and herbs, were found in man's realm of earth, and Odilon Redon painted them just as he had seen them in the meadows or under the summer skies.

This painter's careful study of nature may seem surprising, because, while everything in the painting "Pandora" may come from the everyday world, the way he has put it together is magical. He explained this by saying that he longed "to put the logic of the visible at the service of the invisible." In other words, he wanted to take the flowers, the butterflies, the

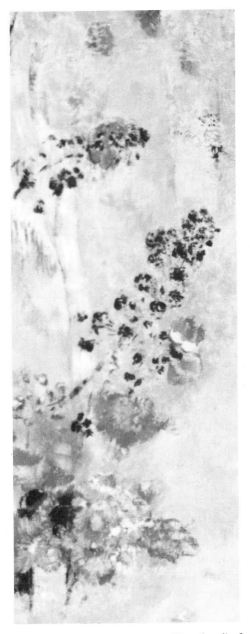

Flowers. Detail from "Pandora" by
Bertrand Jean (Odilon) Redon.

plants on earth, paint them just as they were, but present them so that they appeared more beautiful, more a part of the gods' world than our own. In this fashion, Redon manages to lift our spirits to those special days when the world does shimmer, when it does excite our imagination and our curiosity. Although the world is always the same, our view of it changes with our mood. On his canvas, Redon tries to bring that mood back, when flowers become masses of colors, breezes a flow of fragrance, and everyone wonders if there could be even more beauty in a little box. Who can blame Pandora? Certainly not the painter.

Odilon Redon created Pandora just as the gods created her in the Greek myth. Her beauty comes not so much from her person as from everything around her. Pandora appears and heightens our enjoyment of the earth. The painter felt this way about his wife, whom he married in 1880. "Without her," he wrote, "what would have become of me? I believe that the yes which I pronounced when we were wed was the expression of the most complete certitude I have felt. . . ." Up to that time, Odilon Redon had worked with charcoal. Because of doubts he created strange beings, dark monsters out of nightmares. After the birth of his son, Ari, in 1889, he turned from black to color, from charcoal to pastels, water colors, and oils, and from nightmares to buoyant visions.

In 1910, the year Odilon Redon created "Pandora," he was enjoying a house in the country, which had been left to him and his wife by her sister. There Madame Redon planted a garden filled with flowers,

Pandora. Detail from "Pandora" by Bertrand Jean (Odilon) Redon.

and her husband painted them from life, delighting in their colors, shapes, and textures.

In this painting Pandora's curiosity is forgiven. The remedy for the sorrows and woes of the world comes from her presence. The first woman brings with her hope.

The Story of Prometheus

𝕫𝕫𝕫𝕫𝕫𝕫𝕫𝕫𝕫𝕫𝕫𝕫

PLATE XII

Once upon a time, there was a race of beings on earth called Titans. They were very ancient and old-fashioned, and one day their sons and daughters rose up and conquered them. These sons and daughters became known as the Greek gods.

A single Titan, Prometheus, managed to live through the battle and escape imprisonment afterward. Though he saw that the new gods were bringing about many needed changes, he did not like their hardness toward men—his creations. The men on earth were struggling. They had no fire. For nine months out of the year, they were cold and hungry and miserable. Prometheus decided to help them. He stole fire from the gods and took it down to them in a stalk of fennel. All at once men's discontent vanished. It was replaced by a wild joy. They had warm houses, hot food, pleasant gatherings. They were also on their way to inventing chariots, plows, and kilns. The earth was humming with work and industry. Soon men forgot to pray to the new gods. They just created a tool whenever something went wrong.

When the king of the gods discovered this, he was enraged. He chained Prometheus to a rock on a lonely mountain as punishment. A vulture came to gnaw at the Titan's liver, which, however, grew back every day. Nevertheless, such a punishment could not go on forever. No one on earth could forget Prometheus. In the end, it was a man, one of the new breed of men called heroes, who loosed the arrow which killed the vulture and set Prometheus free.

The modern Swiss artist, Kurt Seligmann, used symbols in his paintings and drawings. Prometheus does not look like a Greek god. His head is bonelike. He comes from the darkness of the past. He lived at the beginning of the world before the Greek gods. He is a strange, unknown being called a Titan.

In the Greek myth, Prometheus was compassionate and intelligent enough to steal the fire and take it down to man. As a result, he was loved by mankind and considered their protector. Kurt Seligmann has taken the ancient Titan Prometheus not just as a symbol of intelligence and fire, but as a symbol of what the two could create. In the story men used fire to create chariots, plows, and kilns. These were the things which made their lives better and led them to live with others in villages, cities, and finally countries. However, as soon as men became creators, they forgot to honor the gods. They forgot to be humble. In this drawing Kurt Seligmann tells what he thinks has happened as a result.

The chariot driver. Detail from study for "Prometheus" by
Kurt Seligmann.

Here Prometheus seems to be part of his mountain. It is not a vulture but a chariot, created by fire and now heading into a vortex of swirling clouds, which is pulling at his liver and tormenting him. The use of fire is bringing endless anguish and possible destruction.

The artist makes this even clearer by hinting at another myth. Once the boy Phaethon begged his father, who was the god of the sun, to let him drive his chariot. The father could not say no. The boy took the reins of the chariot and was unable to control it. The chariot went straight into the sun, caught on fire, and fell in many pieces to the earth.

In the drawing, the driver is having as much trouble keeping his chariot under control as Phaethon. A vortex opens below as he turns against his enemy. Prometheus has the stalk of fennel in one hand and a shield on his arm. His weapons seem a part of him and he in turn is part of the earth. Will he survive? The magnitude of their struggle is stressed by the restless lines and sudden, black marks which are part of this artist's powerful style.

Kurt Seligmann said that his fascination with symbols came with his fascination with carnivals when he was a child in Switzerland. His symbols travel down the centuries like those carnivals. Prometheus is an ancient symbol of fire and intelligence. Phaethon is the symbol of ignorance and haste. The chariot is a creation of fire. Kurt Seligmann has retold the story of Prometheus with deep feeling for the challenges confronting the modern race of men.

Prometheus. Detail from study for "Prometheus" by Kurt
Seligmann.

About the Author

PENELOPE PRODDOW was graduated from Bryn Mawr College where she received her degree in Classical and Near Eastern Archaeology. She is an alumna of the American School of Classical Studies at Athens, and the author of *Dionysos and the Pirates; Hermes, Lord of Robbers;* and *Demeter and Persephone.* The idea for this book grew out of her Sunday lecture program, "Art Tells a Story," in the Junior Museum of The Metropolitan Museum of Art in New York City.